AF825289

The Sufferings of Light

For Robert K. Wallace,
in gratitude for the
Third Matheson Seminar
in Comparative Arts
St. Louis
March 13, 2000

Robert E. Hegel, Chair
Comp. Lit. at Wash U.

The Sufferings of Light

William H. Matheson

Selected Poems

P.S., A PRESS
Middletown Springs, Vermont
1996

Some of the poems in this volume appeared previously in *River Styx*, in various editions of *Anthology* (Ikuta Press, Kobe, Japan), and in *Tung Ch'i-Ch'ang's Album*, a 1995 limited edition of one hundred handmade books designed and published by Tom Lang of Art Motel Press.

Set in ITC 11/14 Galliard, a type modeled after the 16th-century French humanist typefaces of Robert Granjon, this book is printed on Springhill opaque vellum, an acid-free stock.

Cover: Detail of a stoneware vase by William H. Matheson
Photograph by Robert Vigiletti

Copyright © 1996 by William H. Matheson
All rights reserved

Printed in the United States of America
Text and cover design by Write Stuff Communications

Library of Congress Catalog Card number: 96-69808
ISBN: 1-889087-01-7

P.S., A PRESS
169 Garron Road
Middletown Springs, VT 05757

Contents

Poems: 1981-1995

Introduction

William Matheson's poetry has had many readers, more, perhaps, than even some of his close friends in this country may realize. For some years, for example, his poems have appeared in a yearly compilation published by the Ikuta Press in Kobe and named simply *Anthology*. The works of five or six contemporary poets, often from several countries, are usually included in each volume, and these volumes are widely circulated and read in Europe and the United States as well as in Japan. Now, with the publication of *The Sufferings of Light*, Matheson's work will reach an even wider audience.

But how is the uninitiated reader to approach work that is at once erudite, passionate, and wryly humorous? In the first place, I believe that, in what I might term a truly Proustian sense, Matheson's poetry is autobiographical. It was, as I seem to recall, the poet himself who some years ago called my attention to *By Way of Sainte-Beuve*, a remarkable collection of memoirs and essays by Marcel Proust. One section in which Proust speaks directly of the true role of the writer sums up beautifully, for me at least, the strategies Matheson has perfected in the composition of his own poetry:

> A book is the product of a very different *self* from the self we manifest in our habits, in our social life, in our vices. If we would try to understand that particular self, it is by searching our own bosoms, and trying to reconstruct it there, that we may arrive at it. Nothing can exempt us from this pilgrimage of the heart. . . . Thus, it is, in fact, the secretion of one's innermost life, written in solitude and for oneself alone, that one gives to the public. What one bestows on private life . . . is the product of a

> quite superficial self, not of the innermost self which one can only recover by putting aside the world and the self that frequents the world, that innermost self which has waited while one was in company, which one feels certain is the only real self.*

Yet even with such a mandate, each poet, each writer must nevertheless choose the materials that serve as a best means of expressing this inner and authentic self. Furthermore, true art, certainly, must be made up of art as well as of individual lived experience, and Matheson's work rigorously intertwines both. As a passionate and discriminating reader, he has consistently chosen from the world he knows best—the world of literature—the building blocks that constitute the structure of each poem. There is, therefore, for the reader, both an element of recognition (that is, an intellectual awareness that an allusion is being made) as well as an element of discovery in virtually every line.

The use of allusion for reinforcement, parody, or extension has been a familiar device, at least in Anglo-American literature, since the appearance early in this century of the work of T. S. Eliot and Ezra Pound, and the same synergies are at work in the poetry of Japan's greatest modern poet, Nishiwaki Junzaburō, some of whose work Matheson himself has translated. If we were to think of a putative model for Matheson's work, however, a still more likely choice would be Stéphane Mallarmé, whose elegant and tightly woven verse defies any adequate translation out of its original French. In the same fashion, the poetry in *The Sufferings of Light* is so remarkably fitted to the English language, or, at any rate, to the

---

* For this citation, see Marcel Proust, *By Way of Sainte-Beuve*, translated by Sylvia Townsend Warner (London: The Hogarth Press, 1984), pp. 76, 79.

writer's own particular poetic use of the English language, that a translation into French (to say nothing of Japanese!) would seem virtually impossible.

In the flow of the lines in each poem in this collection, then, there are blocks of words that seemingly represent for the poet elements of prior meaning (although these meanings too may shift and turn through their new juxtapositions). These *objets trouvés* spring not only from the poet's reading, but also from his experience as one who loves music and the visual arts. Consider his references to Haydn [p. 38] and Schubert [pp. 94, 97] and to the modern Italian painter Giorgio Morandi [pp. 70-74]. Indeed, the poet's own work as a potter must have taught him—and from a new and evocative perspective—something about the processes and travails of artistic creation in a plastic mode.

Since his reading has occupied the space of so many years, and has been so personal, so demanding, and so eclectic—in the most fearless sense of the word—it seems doubtful that many, if any, of his readers will catch all of his elusive and many-layered allusions. It may be enough, rather, to know that, whether direct or oblique, these many and varied allusions have been chosen as the building blocks for the poems themselves.

Through and around these multilayered blocks flows the swift current of Matheson's own poetic sensibility. By juxtaposition, humor, lyricism, even parody, the lines are swept along, piling up one on another, as the poet moves toward expressing that "self in solitude" of which Proust so eloquently speaks.

Some of Matheson's references to art and literature are quite specific, and this suggests, to me at least, that an intellectual recognition on the part of the reader will enhance their value within the larger structure of the poem. When, in the sequence "*'Nous, les indiscrets,'*" the poet mentions "Gilles" [p. 52] a few lines after mentioning a "pilgrimage to

Cythera," he pulls in the whole bittersweet quality found in those two great Watteau paintings. Similarly, a "Wozzeck moon" [p. 37] in the sequence "Eye scarcely opens" extends the lyric thrust to encompass the striking, horrible moment in Act III of the Alban Berg opera *Wozzeck* (based in turn on the Georg Büchner play) in which, when Marie is murdered, the orchestra chillingly describes the rise of a "blood-red moon." And of course, there are the references to Vermeer's "expected yellow" [p. 73], which conjure up the death of Bergotte in Proust's own masterpiece, *Remembrance of Things Past.*

Whatever role music may be assumed to play in these poems—and that role is a great one—no figure seems more present than Franz Schubert, and in particular his great song-cycle *Winterreise.* The phrase "*wunderliches Tier*" occurs more than once in these poems. In the original, the line is "*Krähe, wunderliches Tier*" (Crow, curious creature), and, in relevant sections of the poet's work, the mysterious crow that haunts the narrator who sings Schubert's "winter journey" seems often starkly present.

Given the range of allusions and themes coursing through these poems, it would be inappropriate for me, or indeed for any one reader, to attempt to rein in by explanation (and so diminish) the flow of the poet's sensibility. Still, it may be useful for me to describe some of the particular building blocks that, even to those well-versed in American and European literature, music, and the visual arts, may still seem obscure.

William Matheson's grasp of East Asian poetry in general, and of Japanese poetry in particular, remains astonishing. His enthusiasms have been such that he took on the not-inconsiderable task of learning elements of the Japanese language itself (both classical and modern) in order to penetrate more deeply into the essence of a poetic tradition that has continued to attract him over the years. Through this effort he has been able to move beyond the kind of generalized appreciation that is possible through reading Japanese verse in translation to a more acute appreciation for the work in the original language, an appreciation that allows him to deal in nuances that may be lost on many of his readers. For this reason, it seems useful to describe some of the references found in the present collection.

Of all the figures who inhabit these poems none is a more powerful presence than the haiku poet Matsuo Bashō (1644-1694), often regarded as the greatest artist in the history of Japanese poetry. Knowledge of Bashō's art, and his artistic persona as well, remains crucial to an understanding of Japanese culture. Indeed, Bashō's own stratagems of self-expression lend to his work a surprisingly evocative character, even in translation. Bashō is a poet who speaks to our own contemporary sensibilities.

The poems in *The Sufferings of Light* suggest that Matheson has movingly overlaid his own sense of poetic vocation with that of this great Japanese poet/recluse/traveler. Indeed, it seems to me that both poets possess many of the same qualities: a sense of the profound danger and darkness to be found in whatever it is we call our human existence, a powerful sense of life as travel, and an ability to find humor in facing all those dangers, a humor that can be at the same time both bracing and delicate. Bashō continued to see life as a journey, and his *Oku no Hosomichi* (*Narrow Road to the Deep North*), published after his death, remains the supreme text of its kind. It is no wonder that it has so often been translated. Several people have remarked to me over the years that, indeed, it had been worth learning classical Japanese simply in order to read Bashō in the original.

Bashō's chosen poetic form was that of the haiku, the seventeen-syllable poem (5/7/5) that, although of lengthy heritage, came into its own in the seventeenth century. There were other great writers of haiku (among them, Yosa Buson and Kobayashi Issa, both of whom Matheson also admires), and the writing of haiku still continues in contemporary Japan. But for Matheson, as well as for most who admire haiku, Bashō remains supreme.

A few comments on the form itself may be helpful. Haiku has a long prior pedigree, developing from the early form of classical Japanese poetry known either as *tanka* (literally, "short poem") or *waka* ("Japanese poem"). The earlier *waka* form was longer than haiku, using thirty-one syllables (5/7/5/7/7). The terms (either *waka* or *tanka*) by which the form was known were presumably developed in contradistinction to lengthier forms of Chinese poetry, which, when imported into the Heian court of the ninth and tenth centuries, helped set artistic taste and standards, particularly those that were included in a series of imperial anthologies, beginning with the *Kokinshū: A Collection of Poems, Ancient and Modern*, a volume assembled about the year 905. Japanese poets of that period often worked in both languages, using Chinese verse forms (and so the Chinese language) for crafting more involved, philosophical statements and using their own native Japanese language for expressing necessarily briefer and more lyrical sensibilities.

The word *haiku* itself is difficult to define succinctly in English. Suffice to say that it is composed of two characters, with *hai* suggesting something amusing, wry, clever, and *ku* meaning simply "verse." The form is so short (beginning, as I mentioned above, as an intentional shortening of the already brief *waka*) that many devices came to constitute important elements in the haiku poet's art: allusiveness, suggestiveness, the power of specific images, and other strategies chosen to maximize the energies available in such a limited linguistic space.

Matheson's collection of poems opens with a *haibun*, which might be roughly translated as "haiku-like prose," a form of densely textured, elegant, and allusive prose writing that Bashō in particular developed as a means to extend the suggestiveness of his individual poems. Bashō also used his *haibun* as a means of weaving individual verses into longer narrative, emotional, seasonal, even spiritual sequences. Matheson's particular form of *haibun* is authentically his own, but whatever his larger purposes in employing the twists and turns of prose as a vehicle for linking and illuminating brief poetic pieces, his use of *haibun* is, nevertheless, reminiscent of that of his Japanese predecessor.

Bashō often wrote linked haiku sequences with students and fellow poets. This was a communal art that drew in turn on another medieval form of Japanese poetry—*renga*, or linked verse. The rules of this art are too complex to set down here (as are the rules for composing communal haiku, which begins with an opening verse—*hokku*—and proceeds through a set of clever rules to produce verbally a sort of theme and variations familiar to us in musical terms from the Mozart and Beethoven models). The flow, the circling back and forth of themes in Matheson's poems, sometimes suggests the model of a *renga* sequence, and it is perhaps not by chance that Matheson much admires a modern set of *renga* poems entitled *Renga: A Chain of Poems*, published in 1971 and written by Octavio Paz, Jacques Roubaud, Edoardo Sanguineti, and Charles Tomlinson. Bashō himself had a number of favorite disciples with whom he exchanged haiku and discussed the nature of poetry. Among them, perhaps the most important was Kyorai, another name the reader will find mentioned in this collection.

Even if Bashō's name were not included, those familiar with haiku would recognize his presence at once. Matheson has included in his *haibun* a mention of a bashō (banana tree) grown by Bashō at his simple hut near Tokyo's Sumida River—but note the wry Handelian reference to an aria containing an homage to a tree from *Xerxes* as well! In "The Golden Larch," Matheson refers to "*furuike* pond," that famous body of water located in what is perhaps Bashō's most celebrated poem:

furuike ya	An old pond:
kawazu tobikomu	A frog jumps in,
mizu no oto	The sound of water

In Matheson's poem the calm surface of the pond mirrors both Bashō's frog and Polyphemus of Greek legend.

Bashō had his own favorite poets, notably the Chinese T'ang Dynasty master Tu Fu (721-770), and, even more particularly, Bashō's great predecessor, the monk and recluse, Saigyō (1118-1190), who lived at the end of the Heian period. Indeed, Matheson has dedicated an entire poem, "For Saigyō," to the latter poet, opening by quoting the thirty-one-syllable *waka*, a work that begins "Shade of willow" and shows the poet so captivated by the sights of nature (the willow, the water) that he stops his own sense of time in order to partake of the power of such beauty. This *waka* by Saigyō was also one of Bashō's favorites and served as model for an imitation/variation that appears in *The Narrow Road to the Deep North*. In this piece, Bashō, too, is struck by the beauty of the spot (he found what was said to be that very same tree seen by Saigyō, or so goes the conceit) but can only stay a shorter time than his predecessor and enjoys watching not the deceptive simplicity of nature but the farm workers busy in the fields:

ta ichimai	One paddy they've planted;
uete tachisaru	Now I am able to leave
yanagi kana	That willow tree!

Bashō's homage is a mere seventeen syllables; Matheson's is

forty lines. Bashō suggests a folk song; Matheson conjures Rilke.

Bashō can combine his references to create a new play between art and life; and in one of his most remarkable passages, a segment from "Bashō: A *Haibun,*" Matheson accomplishes the same thing by juxtaposing images drawn from three separate haiku of the master [p. 6]. Matheson's lines read,

Akashi skylark,
In a helmet, cricket's song,
The fields of winter.

The middle line is taken from a particularly moving haiku in which Bashō, on one of his trips, was shown a touching relic, the helmet of the aging medieval warrior Saitō Sanemori, who dyed his hair so as to appear young enough to join in battle:

muzan ya	How pitiful!
kabuto no shita no	Beneath the helmet
kirigirisu	A cricket sings.

Matheson's three lines are an integrated whole, yet each line is further enriched by the complexities expressed in its previous assemblage. Surely this collage represents, in a brief space, one of Matheson's most suggestive poetic accomplishments.

Along with Bashō, there are other figures in the history of the Japanese arts to whom Matheson has been attracted. Like Yeats and Claudel, two Western poets whom he admires, Matheson has found himself drawn to the spare and evocative medieval Noh drama, which combines masks and faces, music and speech, dance and gesture. His mention of "crystals in Zeami's bowl" [p. 92] refers to a striking line in "Notes on the Nine Levels," an early-fifteenth-century treatise on acting by the great actor, playwright, and theoretician Zeami Motokiyo (1363-1443) in which the dramatist refers to one of the highest levels of performance as "snow in a silver bowl." In more general terms, the elegance and probity redolent of the Noh theatre pervade many of Matheson's most elegant lines.

There are also reflections throughout this collection of the poet's study of the Japanese language and of his travels in Japan. He mentions Shiga Bay, so filled with poetic associations in classical *waka*, and of the deer in Nara, who still roam the beautiful park in which the most ancient and striking temples and shrines can be found. His mention of the "godless month" [p. 44] refers to the month in the traditional Japanese calendar when, according to legend, the Shintō gods leave the ancient land of Yamato to visit the shrine of Izumo on the remote Japan Sea. *Keshiki wa miezu*, he writes [p. 15], "I cannot see the scenery," and the phrase takes on a poignant energy within the contours of the whole poem. It is perhaps inevitable, too, that the famous phrase of renunciation, *shikata ga nai* ("there is nothing to be done about it"), should also appear [p. 61].

Matheson's ever-increasing love of Chinese art and poetry is also apparent in this gathering of his work. Among the references woven into the poems can be found a mention of the T'ang poet Wang Wei (701-761), one of the earliest and greatest of the Chinese poets who viewed nature through a new and transcendental Buddhist framework [p. 12]. The Southern Sung painter Ma Yüan, who lived at the end of the twelfth century and who was so much appreciated in Japan, also makes an appearance [pp. 67, 92], as does the supreme calligrapher of the Ming Dynasty, Tung Ch'i-ch'ang (1555-1636) [pp. 53–63]. The innovative poet of the Northern Sung, Lin Pu (967-1028), is briefly mentioned as well [p. 58]. If their cumulative presence is perhaps not as great as those of Bashō, Zeami, Saigyō and the others, the level of transcendental elegance these Chinese poets contribute to the world of Matheson's more recent work remains equally striking.

One of the later poems in this present collection is entitled

"Framing Is All." In one sense, it seems to me that so much of William Matheson's passionately affirmed connections with the artists of the past provide him with a means of establishing with precision each frame needed to enable his readers to experience the exquisite details—personal, artistic, literary—from which these poems are constructed and to look beyond those details toward the depths they plumb.

In the end, for me, these poems, while unmistakably the work of a poet of wide learning and intellectual sympathies, are also the work of an artist who believes in the power of art as affirmation. William Matheson's work can thus serve as a means, sometimes steady, sometimes strangely unsettling, of repossessing those transcendental passions that we too may once have experienced but whose recurrence only high art can stimulate, can give. And, by serving that function, the poems in this collection become high art in and of themselves.

University of Pittsburgh J. THOMAS RIMER

Bashō: A *Haibun*

"Mais enfin la main se décide," as, how many years from now, *ce cher* Valéry will say, "Finally, the hand makes its choice; and, just like the player cautiously venturing a card upon the table or moving a piece on the chessboard, we launch—against immanent purity, against the integrity of the possible—an attack (word, line) which breaks the spell."

Void of the white page
Nothing more beautiful than
What does not exist.

That at least is done, the spell—as who should say—broken. It was never merely the actual writing, the actual getting it on paper, that exhausted me (poor aging unicorn, worth less than a broken-down horse): it was, really, that writing meant seeing and seeing meant travel and travel—especially, I find, after that debilitating trip to the Northern Provinces last year—has a tendency to remove one from home and from . . . things. . . . From one in particular:

Wind, in your great leaves
Harp, in the green of your heart
I sit beneath you.

I speak of my tree, my banana tree, my *bashō.*

Gales rip leaves to fans
Your phoenix tail is shattered
Useless, glorious.

Is it not, this conflict between staying and going (oh, I was eloquent, on that last trip, about "travel as a cosmic motif"—it's likely to become an anthology piece—or, if you will, between writing and not writing—all in a name? Take, for example, "Matsuo Bashō." "Matsuo" is full of princely pinetrees, flags flying, hair in the wind (there also hangs a tail): the whole induces to movement, flight, escape, wandering, indeed to Matsushima, the goal of my last excursion:

Rampant grey couchant
. . . to rally all that remains . . .
Island white body.

While the other, "Bashō," clearly says I should stay here with my tree:

Fire in a row
Grass with serpent turned to art
Antiquated bird.

Which, in sum, means that the things of this world suffice; the very things around me suffice, suffice to tell us that all is celebration and deprivation. My tree—*ombra mai fu*—has nondescript flowers and its wood is good for nothing: it is lament and ode. Salvationwise, it is a sinful attachment—"firmly tied to the passions like a yak to its tail"—but then, so is travel. And poetry.

Poetry, in these brief forms we seem condemned to cultivate, inspired by, contingent upon, or even totally divorced from travel, is—the notion is necessarily puerile—voyage, of a perilous sort, and quest, more, conquest of nothing by something:

White space, magic mirror,
Soul, place where signs and lines give
Birth to miracle.
Faced with fatality the
Brush is tensed, is paralyzed.

(That again being Valéry, which proves that even hermetic utterance can be, how shall I say? condensed, if it turns prolix; one wonders if somehow the goal of *tanka* and haiku be not to transform Valéry into Mallarmé? Or, if not into Mallarmé, at least into something more urbane:

Ce toit tranquille, où marchent des colombes,
Entre les pins palpite, entre les tombes;
Midi le juste y compose de feux
La mer, la mer, toujours recommencée!
O récompense après une pensée
Qu'un long regard sur le calme des dieux!

Thus:

Roof-top, swaying doves
Pines and tombs with gleam between
Sun half-run turns flame
To ever Sea ever new!
Thought's prize: eyes on gods' calm rest.

I've always wanted to get my hands on Swinburne. . . .)

That phrase, "the conquest of nothing by something" (I must ask Kyorai about it; now *there's* a person you can talk poetry with!): how fearful that nothing!

What sacred from all
Beauty emanates, forbids
    Our touch, blights gesture?
Suspended in an action,
We have come to fear ourselves.

How utterly inadequate that something!

    Flies flock to whiteness,
Swarm and riot—nuptials, games—
    Virgin, corrupted.

Any poem is just *barely* there, just *barely* saved! And by what we call a poet who, if he manages to exist at all, knowing what he does, must be the world's most resistant thing, with a diamond edge. For he rescues what? What are his hostages? What his booty?

    Akashi skylark,
In a helmet, cricket's song,
    The fields of winter.

Merely to say that today's light has a certain color—what could be easier than to describe light?—to what anguish of circumlocution, to what agonies of paraphrase, to what torments of the *à peu près* are we subjected?

    No: I cannot seize
This rime, this ice, this freezing
    Crisis light on trees.

(. . . .)

Sequences: 1978–1987

This well burning red

This well burning red
drops from it round in waters
light through the blinds blinds

        aging ageless in a room
        spurious paralysis

take up from under
tree now vertigo of green
vitreous to verse

        sunsets stroke the grain of oak
        out upon it hand of me

of you wasting light
future your going present
your past having gone

        what time when time whether time
        drops from it round in waters

glows golden from stone
how should the dead not quicken
flower paint ensouls

        cut frees crystal from the brute
        fire freezes clay in form

this well burning red
thunders are engaging it
creux toujours futur

empty steps in water's heart
pasos de un peregrino

of you wasting light
this body seen by phosphors
prospers and goes out

mine in mines of solitudes
"annals diaphanous wind's"

cat growls to darkness
yellow convent eyes through fog
hides his head in me

who wander in these leaves this
house deceives night by day by

opening of wings
I regard moth regards me
close-breathing wings close

"grief of things that I know not"
la casa tan querida

light through the blinds blinds
morning frosts black to argent
prospers and goes out

lightnings smite all fireflies
might transfix each fish of pond

luz tú vertical
ore in these lemons blazing
glows golden from stone

how should the dead not quicken
shred of Heian in brocade

aux baumes de temps
prelude for a final fugue
when time whether time

drops from it round in waters
blurring your averted eyes

face beyond my mind
future your going present
sun in your eyes lies

mutes heart mutes tongue mutes sorrow
all our nights' obscenest birds

no: sing stone sing tree
water sing fidelity
whippoorwillfully

submerged to depths of branch now
evenings utter treasury

why when wind extorts
this ah! do gods desert our
cruel radiance

silver idol eye of gold
streetlight convent morning fog

of you wasting light
"ecstasy the lute's third verse"
Yao Shou's tower burns

drops from it round in waters
tornano al centro i sassi

change not this vantage
sun through well through water glass
light through the blinds blinds

downwards falls on hand on oak
clay on ash flow lava smoke

modulate too late
or even early riot
pinecones crash on moss

tree now vertigo of green
Wang Wei's garden in the soul

river deer drink dawn
enters sun o galliard
this solemn step this

well-burning well burning red
drops from it round in waters.

The Golden Larch

(Pseudolarix amabilis)

Tell me of distance
word spread like honey on field
what other save light

    high translated to the larch
    upmost loved is utmost fraud

move more west to oak
comes no wind to violate
Dodona's treasury

    now strain to hear the color
    watch to blindness every sound

sun superfluous
from within so fire comes
maple in my hands

    Pascal's lesson: leave no room
    bend the knee asperge believe

water to such use
elemental sacrilege
out of the credo

    rocks at least are endlessly
    leopards absorbing noontime

a calm a partage
"melancholy and copper"
voice resolved to voice

to thickness of this quiet
dark enough for plangency

stones with water glaze
decay cicadas' cadence
diminuendo

help me deaden every sense
you my golgothas of heart

ténèbres d'Egypte
street meeting defeat retreat
annihilating

void persists *penser peser*
gravity were lighter sheer

leaping this night arch
upwards vaults to recollect
larch when sea subsides

to fall before the autumn
fraudulent who lures our love

indite you message
alike for self and other
eye will noways seek

presence yet will stamp its seal
end of night *Gebrauchsmusik*

say something simpler
"grammar offers pavilions"
tentatively larch

hear how rain preludes itself
hear what happens after rain

hear my watching you
hear what suicidal light
larch leaves entorches

hear how *furuike* pond
is mirror for Polyphemus

dignify a prose
commemorate the common
excommunicate

extirpate deracinate
the perjured Hellenistic

(late) *mon innocence*
commence à me peser say
rather massive now

silver gilds this bronze of me
god whatever God am I

with us abiding
denn es will Abend werden
loving hiding larch

moribund September voice
keshiki wa miezu

no sign seen of it
waters daily sheen more rare
notwithstanding air

larch bends yellow in my thought
who have forgot the colors

words their flowers have
all her virtue half his life
raped or dead to be

one and thirty syllables
in a courtly *florilège*

"poetry is nouns
used caressed abused betrayed"
waylaid arrested

we at best to madness led
desolation celebrate

alone or where no
sun is panoply is shield
on his field is field

word of distance honey light
larch most lovely larch most false.

Wait you cannot count

Wait you cannot count
what color here is squandered
on your dulling eye

        who only see ice forming
        in the veins of leaves of words

is soul poniarded
is every tree a judas
versed in betraying

        the water burns a krater
        of the sun *le beau mensonge*

lie with me a while
or "For God's sake, sit with me!"
Mandelstam's lips move

        still to after rend this noon
        to stillness: *Licht war: Rettung*

koto in maple
branches each its notes on mirror
consanguinity

        of muscat grapes of goldfish
        of larch by moon ignited

single benighted
some voice of cricket something
here petitioning

prison for us both my dear
raging prism schism-year

interrogation
shining Grand Inquisitor
wield now sun and shield

Armageddon vintager
flailing oaks to nudity

glorious nothing
excellence signaling void
rare meaninglessness

tenth month hecatomb of air
I cannot breathe this fire

pillagers gleaners
my brush a rootless flower
black phalanx starlings

moving warp my hair is white
I am still illiterate

psalm to remembrance
salvation is memory
but what remember

nothing then outflames this now
salamanders cannot burn

these will not be told
leaves are mordents *ports-de-voix*
toccata of rain

no it is only rain no
only leaves only what is

only saffron massed
in the east there lacquered rich
a box lid opens

later leads to frost of lead
the cat's fur melts in my hands

he has lain amongst
chrysanthemums he reeks of
spices and of dark

signal shadows on the fence
Bergotte dying Vermeer's Delft

accidental day
modulates to flat sea wind
sharp hawthorn branches

chosen this were mystic's way
grace were irresistible

undeserving we
are swerving things *che mai non
fur vivi* curving

what of mind remains to me
to these my midnight fervors

moonlit words to fog
congeal a love a winter
claw upon my heart

I would explain to you this
sudden stun this sunless thud

but you distracted
godlike attend I venture
to Schubert listen

weeks were harvest months a trove
"seldom, especially now"

when is this the first
or uttermost of bareness
I remember shores

gaunt with wreckage cargo chests
split open surf in bronze clanged

down fall this solving
nascent snow slow dissolving
all absolving all

wait count what color here is
squandered on your dulling eye.

Simply it is wind

Simply it is wind
on water wind on water
water only pond

hiding no known mystery
water wind and leaves from tree

this were scarcely scene
baroquely to be gilded
wind by water chilled

it I mostly mean the sun
high in paucity just in

noon not withstanding
wind changes little barely
it lies on water

while this so posthumously
late in night would tell us wait

only water means
and means no more than water
in all its turnings

learn its brutal essences
lesson cruelly got by heart

rest assured the rest
will flow as this flows slowly
down this trunk of tree

this beauty crux or body
being what you will in rain

nature's straightest line
declines "one inch of longing
one inch of ashes"

somewhere smokes in sunshine jade
stone seems here to sire mist

no enough of this
Mohn und Gedächtnis sublime
meter is sacred

being as it were a stroke
ink raven on parchment frost

holding water serf
you see it all escape us
even tied to form

consider ice: seal upon
seal a silkworm spins demise

hemlocks in glaciers
plum spray in devotion prays
pearls wax to the moon

"embalmed with eternity"
will theme bear variation

stones grow old mists age
water glows to reverence
trees to sanctity

so why then drop on sleeves these
tears like crystalizing fog

through which on window
moon knighting water blazes
him *chapelle ardente*

Sénanque and arching voices
fall back to the pool of mind

this disposition
sun now laid upon the moon
cynosure myself

yellow lights on white *ce cler*
luisant . . . ce neigeant flocquant

should lead you to my
(mad) request but only leads
to my slow turning

glance through glass from east to west
witnessed witness witnessing

there is no one here
but wind whose so soft skin no
frontier guard of Silk

would turn back barring passage
wind on water simply wind

through trees among grey
morning would be indiscreet
light a blasphemy

"innocencie columbine"
wavers on the "whirlpool's lips"

it lies on water
will theme bear variation
only water means

whosoever seek its aid
. . . *chi dal delfino aita* . . .

the heart its pleasure
judge by pleasure of the eye
its reasons having

eddies and leaps reposes
beats in silence sudden stares

itself transposes
to leaves from trees to water
modulates to wind

daily grasp less more deeply
this so posthumously late.

Note night soundlessness

Note night soundlessness
chrysalis for moths of words
would have us winter

    strips down to marble body
    greased with ice our touch would melt

but here is thawing
pines revolve each on axis
spins planes of green slide

    verdigris on Carthage bronze
    copper where a horse still runs

what to say of stone
color of late persimmon
fruit late in the year

    deserted but for sun we
    wonder how this fugue persists

why its compassion
when its voices color rare
fruit late in the year

    while buildings slip to evening
    what blank in pines when rain stops

till then not noted
how fire makes shining black
night note soundlessness

track it out from room to room
panthers we in case of snow

"cannibals of hearts"
desertion by us of us
what this but foretaste

like seaweed in salt-fires
sun burns of a morning ice

coruscates a moon
seeing remembers later
night is day relived

what will be the future's hail
seen from the side to roundly

fall in the cat's-eyed
signs of worldliness of love
of apprenticeship

while buildings slip to evening
"ces édifices qui chantent"

mute before such white
shadings infinite of shade
deafened faced by black

track it out from room to room
zones of soundlessness round us

thing beyond a grasp
water hangs on hawthorn thorns
Teika in the snow

swirling knows aging no one
comes nor has one where to go

opulence of grey
enrolls us unrolls us scroll
charcoal inks in tree

cedar bleeding in the sleet
"lovely enchanting language"

tundra barrens waste
translating to saintliness
dying in eclipse

unfound elusive rusty
sounds crows rising in maelstroms

oak leaves clack in wind
no I only hear the heart
blood sings litany

opens rose inside the soul
chaconne of Buxtehude

ripe late in the year
but what is the single word
wunderliches Tier

thing beyond a grasp to sing
hemlock's green fioritura

desperate morning
sun returns upon his shield
what this but foretaste

touched by the wings of madness
of my body what is left

night soundless rounds us
sparks to canticles ascend
ashes crash to ash

heat if we could capture it
fire if we took within

arcana of light
chrysalis for moths of words
we late in the year

wonder how these strings consort
what blank in pines when rain stops

coil of garden rocks
embroidered silk at midnight
futile o the voice

shifting suddenly shadows
soundlessness rounds us night note.

Listen beyond me

Listen beyond me
lie acres writhing in wind
furling old rivers

    now that the sun has faltered
    touch the nearly lemon light

always as if last
morning letter to the self
in thraldom to what

    ever dawns inside the eye
    ever preludes in the ear

nightfire sired
testify the birth of tree
écarte la lampe

    inkwell crystal consciousness
    drop of shadows relative

to something's being
forest horror thunder mute
scattered within leaves

    expanse of wood before me
    grain of it caresses hand

draw from heart a sun
call up spring by sheerest will
chastely these eclogues

but where is mine within this
which alien voice is mine

what raving hemlock
through a window to tower
turns in the wind blue

"grasses of Forgetfulness"
thornbushes of broken strings

the late sonatas'
violence: no: think rather
willows card the sun

what would move us from this place
horizon like Medusa

turn eye to stone to
water sacrificial wind
to geese under moon

under the surface treasures
of minimal gold blossom

sprout through the water
ton souvenir en moi luit
comme un ostensoir

monstrous shows how highest art's
composed of least with frenzy

tracked to wretched lair
tortured it capitulates
wags its tail and fawns

"them I would perpetuate"
my fabulous my senses

what dearth transmuted
leaves what residue of dearth
ô sûr châtiment

volcano through the grape skins
evening turning ash and gold

this Thames of Whistler
"eyes in last extremity"
this most vaguely sketched

no the sky is all of light
black so lucid never seen

morning in a fog
painted by who might it be
passing through a dream

looms oak loom hemlocks hawthorn
these the deities of place

who seize us seizing
them in all their solidness
we their fragile poem

look to a grey being born
look to a dying of black

if we were to walk
tonight beside this water
obligatory

links in sequences assail
our sight impale our failing

ear flail touch avail
no serpent-slaying cedar
no balm specific

suddenly I shrink afraid
before the moon's glissando

I would speak of far
light late lost in the trees' voice
blindness in water

desolation celebrate
what little amid age lasts

wine cast in the sea
save in dream too dim recalled
memory's decades

hazards of our Lazarus
vernal bodies burning grass.

Tell of light the source

Tell of light the source
here where only crystal shores
water's ghost on walls

    "as drops seeping to the roots"
    what cleaving inwards the heart

fills crypts its beatings
"words confused the stars besiege"
east is cloth-of-gold

    here where water falls in light
    cleaving what stilled inwards voice

attend most chiefly
almost night it flames in wind
a well burning red

    all to be resolved is this
    by ground and its divisions

will a last of sun
claw me clutch me take me up
no prayer is nothing

    only what the water's flow
    knows only what rain's veils know:

is it wind or night
"axioms of crepuscule"
boats to harbors turn

wake the cliffs beneath my feet
far different is my minstrel

the lake his lute frets
moon nor chalice nor monstrance
souvenir en moi

some squandered coinage outcast
golden prodigality

seed but from which god
from dark to dark through shadows
fecundates an eye

of this void this coquetry
"mind must east itself, find Sun"

find cleaving inwards
as drops seeping to the roots
like waves beneath me

hollow out the very rock
turn foundation into lace

translate me the moon
words were long used up for so
high argent blizzard

snow cannot abide such heat
cleaving inwards seeping drops

now quiet thickens
will our mansions all endure
will flesh will spirit

far from water substance fails
drops seep inwards cleave the heart

hawk against the sun
wind or waves in cedar grove
hover love move cove

smell of sun at noon in trees
flagelated by a wind

craves to touch my face
rages to a gold a green
now desolation

tell me what I see of trees
of two trees what behind them

roaring to the front
some Heraclitus-river
"moons rise on mid-noon"

light glancing off to sheerness
light shrill bludgeons fawning day

has nothing taken
place becomes a sense of place
times time yields prison

what would body ever know
save cleaving inwards heartwards

home where windows wait
stones decline a sun who falls
my lamp's bright wasteland

beauty like a stone is cold
strikes us like a silence dumb

words come more slowly
eye more slowly sees the sun
cleaving inwards heart

but outrage of the maple
devil's advocate belies

turning to a dark
psalm-chanting "song of degrees"
. . . rally what remains . . .

had you promised only jade
had you forgot my sorrow

voice in the heart stilled
against the light cleaves inwards
tell of all its source

martyr makes me holy sun
seeping to the roots as drops.

Eye scarcely opens

Eye scarcely opens
sight is all divining blank
only the house breathes

    why is spirit so shattered
    what will compensate for fog

being strives to think
what is left from light extract
love the floor I pace

    harden ear to choicest voice
    deafen hand to merest touch

mes sens fabuleux
but what should this be aimed at
what hypostatize

    arrest or carve in some wise
    overweening form or vise

eye scarcely opens
spring through film of hawthorn branch
drowning Wozzeck moon

    late a thunder late a train
    tells its syllabary beads

nights beyond account
agon with absent angel
forcing the sun's halt

lancé du fond d'un naufrage
this will dull the casual glance

still the water's still
words within the lists of love
are sometimes entered

yet this cooling spring obtains
my saying and gainsaying

Haydn his trio
sounding us this day of ash
to rain's *fugato*

dead must be to hear no rain
nor cleave apart at voices

ones mostly lying
mostly swirling ice in glass
mostly daily yours

enough you wax by anguish
most particularly mine

leave me to this black
light causes sickly thriving
panache above all

shearing air young maple leaves
but what if this lacked meaning

in itself or in
whichever way we thwart it
eye scarcely opens

closes swarthy on evening
should a drop of water slide

down an iris blade
essence would be seized in ink
on silk or paper

leads to letter mine to you
o what waste inheres herein

coda epilogue
to no preceding movements
all's lost when music's

solely heard on space alone
rests hand senses die unshared

"fingers of the sun"
wait for the poplar to calm
what living persists

for pigeon's cry to quiet
what no longer touches ear

sequenze chemins
the thick of sound it might be
that we would rival

the allatonceness of it
pilgrimage through time of paint

take up the triptych
water being only theme
variations light

here sun and pond and lilies
leave behind umbrageous love

shading filter screen
for talking writing craving
lexicon body

unworthy of all richness
digne d'un trésor quelconque

Cloud of Unknowing
pass between the source and us
forcing the sun's halt

while rains of moon flood terrace
attend all spheres of silence

night enumerate
think fresco fugue plinth granite
on water's muscles

on hemlock's ode on wind-red
maple eye scarcely opens.

Heavy of lightning

Heavy of lightning
air will die for lack of air
cleanse o bolt the heart

morning enters imposter
what for a day might this be

topicality
changes of the seen occlude
"sorrows, pallid moon's"

here there is some nightlong bird
here sun takes shape wind colors

windows on water
frame for my epiphany
flight to what from what

hill ebbs elms flow neap spring flux
body shines through mind as proof

take this where sun dies
gasping ravening my skin
he to words subsumed

to where beyond you air dies
airless no: rip-tide in grass

water evoke it
on this sheerest blade of land
what more main than fog

morning and I turn to rock
see how book becomes a light

in dürftiger Zeit
will thirst make chasm fruitful
die for lack of air

weeks we have been rich in them
how prodigy our squander

waste become hall-mark
paper yellowed turns reproach
any ink will do

what the fault that all defaults
anecdote some other world

not that the flesh feeds
not that there we swarm in plot
not that the months freeze

try novelties of daylight
vista alternate or pose

how could this ravish
when did mind be triumph's slave
whom could crush this voice

others' jubilate god wills
air will die for lack of air

Gobi utter rich
"nothing will have taken place"
bring alp to Eden

expatiate on stunning
while September rain explains

something yearly comes
as comes the nearly color
over-weening larch

I think the central image
shone like stones beneath water

and has persisted
to this book in iron bound
"days become moments"

as though some febrile mission
epic triviality

rather simplified
infiniment sur la terre
frenzy of a grail

burned me to a single word
burned you to a single shape

cube cylinder brass
"future ripens in the past,
sees the past decay"

will air die for lack of air
will here be where snow gently

drops to standing pools
expatiate on stunning
cold behind the eyes

numbly feels or through an ice
the godless month October

air lacking air dies
promulgates severity
chains us to simple

antiphons of Venice sun
afternoons deflecting pond

look leaves of weight sink
freighted for excavation
hawthorn falls to roots

elements survive debacle
water fires earthly air

dying does not die
evidence this screen on screen
of green as west grows

furious against failing
neither word nor clay betrays.

Tend me to blackness

Tend me to blackness
light without lens is halo
splintered through a rose

        trees if they march on house
        let them enter they are theirs

stone takes possession
by mortmain or defaulting
hemlocks are ensconced

        sleet fleetly would invade us
        wind blinds convent's every eye

barring act of grace
why should this quick turn to words
lacking it may be

        any claim to clang of bronze
        any renaissance of sun

for winter's tyrant
mammoth-heart in amber-ice
mind a glacier moves

        only writes in certain light
        but what if day-down knives us

north: Kyoto lingers
why should only color save?
east: planes mildly Greek

south ah south the wonted gold
west transmogrified by elms

and this how comes it
that fates from all four quarters
met wove saw to it

that someone here be seated
seated here and see to them

become their object
it is excursus over
scooped out of a well

this so early waterlight
green after midnight become

winter of desert
wind as though it were a spring
two months early drunk

staggers from arch and river
rhododendrons climb the walls

so for a seen change
passamezzo of our waves
under passagework

a flight of yellow parrots
daily with varied repeats

gulf-wind will madden
what does it what does it want
it wants sand and self

surf and the self burning beached
sun brittle sybarite light

thinking it wants not
nor memory to pale us
brutish servitude

one has seen an appletree
lording it snow still on branch

or lifting my eyes
from Bashō trekking northwards
tremolar de la

marina green above lawn
where voices sing with organ

think deeply on fog
but why does hand no more move
on paper engulfed

think that it is analogue
as if that were some solace

winter absconding
(if poem ends whiteness returns)
saves us for summer

does it burn us to beauty
reduce us to sheer meter

no: we are countless
will flesh find flesh in wreckage
trove will we become

yes but not like sheen of wind
not like high glintings of wind

sparse new year savings
here where the "courts of the sun"
breaking seclusion

have moved to new Capitals
leaving jade rubbish behind

or if it darkens
or if dark is merely prose
bleak banality

what "event dearer than gold"
might goad us ("after the moon

has set, the desk's four
corners") to enter on wind
piercing black channels

mind achieves its mindlessness
words sound distantly Soundwards.

"Nous, les indiscrets"

Words in place reside
(in us no surely never)
site is lexicon

        brightness in all directions
        yet black the ink that spells it

this in answer to
a plethora of questions
I have failed to ask

        notwithstanding contretemps
        sun at its grandest arrest

sun merely stands there
sphere hesitates above ray
eidolon cultless

        yet declines is declining
        in nondescript excrescence

cloud quatrefoils it
sense that rain splinters dry planks
retreat inwardly

        to the east explodes the light
        redemption *feux d'artifice*

moronic beacon
set in motion by some dead
pointedly pointless

I wander cardinally
asking what of all the nights

now that tempests cease
now that all rushes to sound
now that is nothing

now that basic numbers fail
now that syllables elude

turn page to terror
avoid it fill its void it
blanchingly stretches

enough indiscretion's goal
theme subject *point de repère*

example Watteau
glimmers galleries afar
sanctified whiteness

arms chastely to sides Pierrot
flat hat perfect fool halo

all untouchables
au-dessus de la mêlée
comedy madness

they display him bedlamite
who displays to some massed crowd

behind us de trop
nous, les indiscrets (sea-gulls
flee our latest storm)

only by his dazzled look
obviates our being here

the scene is elsewhere
we exiled or we the scene
we disinvited

Pierrot content laughs beyond
us and the ladies and lutes

abstinence of mind
pilgrimage to Cythera
or *feste galante*

look so ocean enspheres us
simplifies us to a clown

monster that is shown
s'il avait l'art de vous plaire
light beyond pine trees

satyr sinister shaded
then at the feet of candor

agon with donkey
proffers with doctor astride
a thwarted meaning

to some other transcending
mind's eye's or eye's mind's seizure

awkward anchorite
between farce and unknowing
fissured through the brain

true sign in all his senses
Gilles has weathered to our clime

pervades these concerts
settings-forth torch-lit sagas
solicitations

embracings threats declinings
charmings arms that grasp a silk

whose evanescence
thunders through grottoes wondrous
forms that turn away

doubtful eclogues serenades
perspectives graceful repose

knows that mirrors give
us indiscreet the little
wisdom we deserve

face seen in morning water
face in breakers shattering.

Tung Ch'i-Ch'ang's Album

I. *Drawing Water in the Morning*

. . . and all this glint advancing
slicing cutting into marsh
varying marginal indentations
short mostly paragraphs
that even deafened eye reads
ear reads or skin reads
even scars in skin read
how "draw" water mornings
or nightwise the night?
surely with gourd pitcher
ewer chalice goblet yes
but go further yes
cursively grassly painting it
graving it, limning it: sleeves'
folds as centuries would have them
inkstone brush sable rat phoenix feather
water for drawing drawing water
but how much water do we draw no
I mean do we sketch no
water in the morning draws this salt
marsh these hidden for all their candor
herons this most blinding grace.

II. *Boneless Landscape*

. . . not so whatever such might be   estuaries at the Sound
even swamps are carapace or   tough molten metal water
mossy back of beached leviathan   is mirroring masts in groves spars
take purchase on the east: "bone structures, rhythmic vitalities"
here are whales that rust in rushes   sails ropes in hopeless bales
hoists that haul or truss them   steamshovel? earthmover? juggernaut?
groaning upright cranes   chewing out a new marina
with girders in their beaks gulls galore   amongst all this some million
as Hart's bridge flashes on our screen   mallards harbor dawn in wings
channels sluices slips rivulets   they gurgle in the moonlight
unassuming bays creeks'   lunatics they chuckle, they coo.

III. *The Long and Winding Stone Steps*

These islanD
Houses gaunT
Even to A
Lack of lovE
Or charitY;
NavicellA;
Great bluE
Ash-grey heroN;
NavicellA;
Dense oveR
Water voiceS
Innocent arC;
NavicellA;
Dense wateR
Innocent archeS;
NavicellA;
Gulls winD-
Surfing oveR
Terns egretS
Osprey-eagleS;
NavicellA;
Eremitic suN
Sets to risE;
Things we sensE
Equate to sucH
Promenades dowN
Steps' windinG.

IV. *Lin Pu's Poetic Idea*

. . . surely it must have had, this "idea," this, moreover, "poetic" idea of Lin Pu's (another Suchow literatus of whom the less said the better) something to do with The Three Perfections? Which are not, as you might think

1) the thickness of night wind rocking this house perched beyond shipyard on a sliver of bog-turf; perversely built to be taken off, once and for all, in the first Major Storm; but hasn't been; wind of the fidelity beacon every twenty seconds grazing us with Law and Order, a green you would not believe it Gatsby light blessing our channel as though some princess oh to hell with it; and other luminescences caught in its web, lighted buoys marking fish nets, monstrous fireflies, stray beams from cars on the highway, various reds flashing danger and where murders have taken place

or

2) drama's sheer banality: that there should have emerged from such blackness this undulating water and land where they touch and become the Elstir other; that every grass is silver, ducks' sheen is Tang porcelain; and, look you! a sailboat just skimming through my porch; I give it coffee and croissants

or

3) this: that all of nature is fuzzy, arc-like, rounded, curved, bodyful, liquid, in the way of becoming something else, motherful, morningful; we others make sharpnesses, verticals, lines across, vectors spartan shaker bauhaus most elegant erect minimal gestures inhuman sparsenesses all too human

but

are

Painting, Poetry, and Calligraphy.

(Tung Ch'i-Ch'ang: ". . . it is a pity the ancients cannot see my version.")

V. *Eight Views of Autumn Moods*

ALEPH:

Force word to paper breath to breathing
  see fields oozing under pressure green
  midnight wrenches out a woodland's groan

BET:

Sound of shadows no the darkness-sound
  lesson shadowed "another autumn
  comes to place its hand across the sun"

GIMEL:

Beautiful enemy savage friend
  turning melisma to litany
  hymn of praise to list of grievances

DALED:

No: but to a heart the sun's dagger
  tempered in September burns me cold
  channel fog will fall in future frost

HEH:

Not "views of autumn" but of its "moods"
  le coeur a ses saisons but autumn
  does it brood on winter, bury spring?

VOV:

Nights grow longer in this very hall
  dust of album leaves ashes of scrolls
  mountains flow like rivers, temples melt

ZAYIN:

What volume cleave to to read by moon
  white medium of understanding
  what book that in the sun is speechless

KHET:

Some simple psalter rune glyph grimoire
  autumn's nightlight will ignite "where there
  is no fire there are no scriptures."

VI. *Warm and Green Layered Hills*

How this title would have been a pretext
for a poem to you I still believed we shared
poetry not realizing the verb was, utterly,
one you were unable to conjugate
had you promised me jade and had forgot, well, that
was admissible but a poem promised and then forgotten no,
shikata ga nai, no way, but how lovely it
would have been "warm and green layered hills"
as a pretext one of so many pretexts for poems to you
I would have begun by citing Keats's "But many days
have passed since last my heart/ Was warm'd
luxuriously by divine Mozart" the heart/Mozart bit
slightly beyond the pale but any Keats is better than
no Keats   no: we're mad, music
is a folly we fondly thought á deux
no poem comes to shore an Herzland
pretexts all come before a text that never came or
are (evasions) (duplicities) (fraudulent enticements)
oh là what a saga we have lived through read
through (since you think "suffering" is "only" text).
We'll no more to the woods
the layered hills are all deforested.

VII. *Casual Writing by a Window*

Casual writing by a window
writing knows no "casual" but
only casualties victims
in a scene prescripted
and "window," mind you!
pure theatre
but begin
in spite
of
what we
know to be
commedia: O
hills' verdant strata
octoform autumn soul
serpentine stairs to Total
Poem on about above upon
this floating house/ water drawn at dawn.

VIII. *Wonderful Conceptions of the Bitter Melon:* A *Haibun*

So "Chinese" this—"Wonderful Conceptions of the Bitter Melon"—someplace amidst misprision, mistranslation, and mystification. Is the Bitter Melon a ***nom de plume*** (***nom de pinceau!***) for some poet-recluse or the name of his abode, studio, salon, cliff-perched hermitage? And wherefore bitter? Its or his "conceptions": free-floating Schwärmerei, alchemical fumisterie? epiphany or legerdemain? To wit:

> Eye is in the skull
>   we will see post-carnally
>   we are our own lamps

Item:
Conceiving of Last Words. Are they privileged? empowered? subversive? marginalized at the center? gender-specific? self-fashioning? self-consuming? self-indulgent? theoretically critical? critically theoretical? life-sustaining? macrophallo-gerontocratic? cuddly?
To wit:

> "Lemonade," Kafka's
>   death-bed scribble, "everything
>   was so infinite."

Item:
Will Folly persist?
To wit:

> Soundswordstranscriptions
>   to gather all that remains:
>   island white body
>   blackbird drowning in the Seine
>   casts of the dice, fauns, these leaves.

Poems: 1981 – 1995

Scroll: After Ma Yüan

Why of a sudden
branches of plum in flower
mere ink upon silk
some poem or other in air

or fitted to rock
earthly and not of earth spray
of words should while hand
the sinister moves outwards

the other clutches
safeguards for recollection
hides in dark brocade
cause the heart as if to say

aux baumes de temps
where dimmer grows chimera
can heart still be said
heard from its western exile

(had you forgotten
had you promised me jade had
you forgotten but
a poem promised forgotten)

APES JABBER IN TREES
GRASS CLOGS HEAVEN'S COURT
DREGS OF WINE HARDEN
INCENSE FROZEN BRONZE

no: see you the soul
knows cleavages and splinters
lattices grottoes
wanders in its bed of stone

and yet is current
somehow would cohere would form
turn torrent to pool
to clarity virgilian

HALL TO SHARDS OF PORCELAIN
WOULD SHAKE IF THUNDERED NOT A
QUIET WHERE THE PHEASANT'S TAIL
SIGNALS ONLY TO OUR EYES

would ask again why
in so thunderous a way
a branch of plum where
black here burgeons to a white

might the eyes in league
with heart incite this blurring
of the sight as if
down cliffs of mind soared river

we know the body
images the waterfall
grows obscure with ink
silently explodes with plum.

The Rothko Chapel In Houston

What to make of black
in all its writhings
rectilinear
to imposition
of its self on self
but lesser as eyes
in this, matching mind,
having left sun pool
and the obelisk
learn virgin to see
how black ignites in
purples shade's lessons
greys in their vaultings
magentas would-be
crimson promises
Tuscany olive
most inner of white.

Giorgio Morandi: Two Paintings

I. *Paesaggio controluce con la casetta bianca*

How are we to say
such burnings against the eye
what if we should say

        subtle but lifelong movings
        minor shiftings of hopeless

flask unpromising
pitcher jug past salvation
what if we should say

        objects cursed to ugliness
        no, worse: things that even seen

as real were never
that but were as if to say
made to be unreal

        their uttermost uselessness
        contrived deprived of any

saving (as they say)
redeeming (as they say) grace
yet grace they say and

        saving what from what they say
        and finally redemption

things that never were
are posited on tables
hypotheses spells

    arcane configurations
    apocryphal alignments

posed in paint thus freed
to fall back to the nothing
they were rescued from

    but in their fall are falling
    before me and beside me

here this almost night
on both sides of a siding
rusting nameless parts

    of parts from god knows only
    what lost late in evening trains

claim direct descent
clamor to be deified
how are we to say

    that tables are horizons
    that Racine wrought these deserts

I *controluce*
walk or undertake to walk
long around a lake

    raked by sundown ice where steel
    or wraiths of steel sprawl haughty

know that theirs is flight
from canvas into slagheap
from rarest choosings

to beatitudes of chance
for nobility persists.

II. *Grande natura morta con la lampada a destra*

Take up signatures
when it appears "Morandi"
grey on grey dissolves

merges watermark paper
a very name is painting

like this wash of trees
most likely olives lined on
table arable

trunks some regulated late
T'ang verse tower turned to vial

glass bread metal knife
early disappear since who
could ever touch them

voice none sings hand none lingers
how are we to say this peace

dark prisons of things
sunt lacrimae but poppies
in a grey vase stop

my heart breathing being stops
flowers too to bronze will turn

amid this muting
of Vermeer a totally
expected yellow

wall than the garden it hides
more beloved as vineless blank

shocks in its candor
so these two orange bottles flail
a failing vision

for the eye to quiet tamed
dulled its grasp to white and brown

or these saltimbanques
amphora goblet ewers
stone-like stones child's ball

cubist tristesse quotidienne
tensed for Rilke elegy

note when pencil just
alights leaves on a snow tracks
we divine as jars

color seemingly de trop
when lines suffice and shadow

alabaster lights
this tabernacle triptych
at the loggia's end

sacred matters we might use
for feastings were we worthy

how are we to say
a sense of world without us
we are their exiles

once all human has been banned
then only lives the human.

Narcissus

This sheet of water lying, pond, myself
or what as such let me contrive to take
is proving in a less than blinding light
a fiction that would cease to gratify

if I: no: words are burdens, weigh down days to
wafers. This sheet of water lying, pond
so clear that moons from Royal Anthologies
are mirrored in its very bed: instead

of that, this sheet of water lying, say,
that taste for ambiguity be slaked,
for what are poems about if not deceit

and gorgeous guile annihilating all
dross dregs slag flesh loss fall waste pain lust void?
This sheet of water. This water. Water.

Winterreise Renga

Day athwart winter
it not we the village leaves
casts off its mantle

        of a sudden wounding pines
        signless wind of after noon

still on hilltop waifs
stretch arms of snow to valley
its ear quite deaf turned

        walls standing speechless and cold
        no: nascent pears load branches

shrill through underbrush
essential delicate witch-
hazel is pending

        bending to the farther bank
        the black makes sandbar of pool

river face of heart
—frozen incised broken ring—
Narcissus plangent

        every movement single sings
        minor chords of memory

castles and seasons
folly light in all its turns
seeing always sea

what then of the beast within
bamboo-burnished white-tail deer

slightest of greenings
crack open limestone ledges
leap upwards leafwords

lone mandarin in frostnight
herons lost light stand on sand

letters only these
barely rarely shadow-lined
nothing to no place

thought were better far from this
o and the grey sundown rains

wunderliches Tier
deer divides the bamboo brake
in flight from Nara

what passions make the beech leaf
cling through snow like shell to reef

sole noises noon on
shallows arrows of geese bark
wild turkeys clatter

here young sun lolls on gravel
stretches to solicit soul

tympanum of quail
coinage along branches bursts
wind legerdemain

paths go nowhere air is all
fall to brooks fool's gold to pools

evening strains to night
river strewn with tombs of light
script looks cryptic-cold

text is woods deceived by spring
decoding knows snow season

body stripped so soon
fast fissure of blackest bird
green more nakedness

leading from the first to this
last burden drone last circle.

Nachtstück

Our inner steeps and shallows slack
upon a time that rain would mask
in somehow much before the moment
surreptitious spring as if
against again the curving inward
stones of castle wall that height
curved outward over us a
cherry tree one stand for all
in foglight were: no better this
flute and chorus drums and pine
reflected in the mirror of wood
a foot were almost moving or
the fan about to fall the sleeve
before the blinding eyes ascends.

Sonus

Night
stays.
Day's
slight
white
rays—
haze—
fight,
lose,
choose
a
new
way
through.

Heron Variations

I

Through water of wood
sounding with eras
heron crosses bridge
some god of the noh
deep in white foldings
each step a motion
canceling movement.

II

Stilt legs lifted
soundless touch sand
drums and flutes cease
beak darts spears fish
frozen we watch
fan cast to floor
—make your heart small—.

III

From this desert of lines
gone from so wide a scene
fleeing so step by step
wood witnesses exit
curtain surprisingly
gaudy rushes upwards
allures engulfs spirits
away this white flower
jutting from a dead tree.

IV

This last lightning lashed the moon
soon God knows what final act
will tactfully have place while
wind gashes face who watches
flail against it masked a white
that quite spent its rhythms sensed.

V

Mid-
night's
whites
grid
bird's
shade
made
words
(glyph
un-
known
if
sun
shone).

VI

Noh by torch
flames the wood
flutes shrive night
finale
heron's dance
exorcized
ghostly wings
wet with grief
crystalized
in pine's dew.

VII

Fold following fold magister
dixit not low country befogged
stone but here some nearly thwarted
moon by twelve-tiered Heian textures
so guile of weaving leads to text
or discourse manifesting bird
algèbre du moi wadingly
waking walking Melancholy
Elegance is this performance
for a court or hamlet dune-lost
head raised maskless eye within turned
to questions of an actor's form
seen from behind where in effect
no audience but self awaits.

VIII

Or from mirador
music of a fallen state
this rondeur sundown
advances to orison
white only surmised
against a blare of water
hesitates by pine
follows bridge to lightlessness.

IX

Black blinds the channel's voice
bespeaking good order
yet what this measured pace
this thinning of darkness
sporadic striations
conjuring up morning
Grace they call it Peerless
Flower future willow's
greening now in past plum.

X

Noon splits
white-robed
demon
idol
doubled
defers
dispels
idol.

Huitains/Octaves: Eight Views Based on Eight Views Based on Eight Views

I

Sunsphere melts to its inverted
pyramid acid etches slate-
grey plate *eau forte fecit Klimt*
it is all *grimoire* these linings
inscribing sound by which I mean
the Sound these around me channels
tracings by ducks drifting sea-weed
maps that the wind makes—"here are whales."

II

A bird behind me telegraphs
a lied posthumously Schubert
almost dark yet water heat burns
but of a wonder vapors rise
mists you would say fogs that nearly
rain scorching on naked bodies
making a sun vague *Untergang*
the night the night will we live it?

III

The sun *en congé* leaves a text
for reflection solitary
reflection: what unknown to me
unimagined unthinkable
warmth of a toughness surging up
in all eventuality
would be abiding should I call
on it to guard against the cold?

IV

Sunday as if to say floating
on these waters floating on sound
wind washing air aria with
variations on a ground light
early already blazing crow's
feathers heron's passacaglia
gulls' hieroglyphic decor for
theatre: to see, seeing, seen.

V

Wren are you wren in my live-oak
mozartizing just after noon
sun sublimating *au couchant*
water to haze apocalypse
frieze of herons as if applied
upon screen of melting goldleaf
your singing is our farthest wind
only you are ice in this forge.

VI

Monastery in the soul built
by who takes refuge there or light
of anchorite: this excessive
tableau verging to total sky
total aroundness as if thrust
of verticality were sin
or tastelessness they are the same
sign utterly of immanence.

VII

What increasingly is blacker
is not only cloud water air
within a room paper I write
upon writing very writing
but even if eye still see them,
still read it: what chilling beacon
will pretend portend transpiercing
the nothingness of human things?

VIII

Point d'orgue this almost will-less wind
crow on the balustrade subsumed
to roiling of wings preened silver-
black silenced closed back oiled with noon
claws as he sidles scrape on wood
minuet his sidelong glance on
my paper a knowing prophet's
"Repent!" but rough with compassion.

Octaves for Madmen

Light is from river's farther bank
tornado's ductile aftermath
in rain webbing cedar branches
Arachne's triumph stuns Wisdom
extravagance of whippoorwill
morse of firefly that all is
(diremore than symbol) signal
green holocaust. *Licht war. Rettung.*

That's past. Words unfreeze a spring branch
down hill disenchanted glacier
catch them in creeks conjugate see
Adam's logos Verbe for making
scene always already as they
tediously say deferred to
some special forest turned backwards
not in time but leaves' undersides.

Poem for you since you bitter sun
write poems for others. Q.E.D.
Thus. And consequently silence
thickly stunning wind is buried
storm here storm there blindness is theme
or rather frogs' ostinato
bourdon passacaglia cadence
falling for an exorcism.

Sole thread in early day's rich stuff
from woods away two argent notes
underweaving understory
underwriting understanding
plot of saga epic figment
am I a god whose sweat is gold
when sunset strikes do we resound
what to what is correspondent.

To nothing nothing light's oblique
slanting to end. No: bird mocking
Schubert what parody by beast
cloud mottles river sloughs its skin
and we wear woven air for sin
is behovely (grayness resi-
due) to river's *sprezzatura*
désinvolture offhandedness.

This now sit with me in blackness
think this numbness that comes upon
lucidity as if dark glass
dumbed even vowels even touching
recite with me harps on willows
or lyres and the cosmic scales
"music for a while shall all your
cares beguile" verse regulated.

Owls hear are scooping out the night
latter wind is river's canyon
sun in ritual confinement
as it were cursed to show itself
today has dealt with winter poems
froststrippedreedswitheredfieldsdawnmoon
tearsonsleevesfreezingrainsdearthof
birds: owls hollowing out the night.

Save beneath cedar hummingbirds
hypostasis of chic and poise
then look: sandbar where yellow
raves *pan de mur* in afternoon
laying about it rich endings
primula they call it goblet
most byzantine or sanctified
as if within a room in Arles.

Rain will have it river rises
woods in connivance knew of it
all afternoon were thick with roar
timbre was low strings deep in timber
birds all engaged in semaphore
chromatic scales square thud of storm
tomorrow is doubtful come ye
wet ye naked upon this ark.

"Friendship is all the house I have"
one wonders why this should be so
or if it be mere text in flux
or sheer rococo-mannerist
adornment of the trivial
a pose to strike or attitude
but what if I had soul all gold
my Callicles? my touchstone, you?

Light is expanding night's chorale
hear fog heaves from the river bed
locusts dead forty years in earth
shed sticky husks and breathe escape
to forty years of death in earth
should we consider stone in all
its stoniness no: better ice
on mountain streams sobbing in rocks.

Trees under between among trees
rain comes to a halt San Marco
of canticle and iconry
mad monk decadent St. Francis
birds eat from the hands of ragged
Des Esseintes who honest daily
toils at Heian verse or how to
English Mallarmé's epistles.

That roar is river under black
some several springs ago it changed
its course proving Heraclitus
but daybreak moon still freezes moves
in waves offshore from Shiga Bay
sing it till it congeals write it
to arrest an evanescence
caress it till it dies as yours.

Tidal wave of oakspray lightning
high wind foundering zenith stops
half-day hiatus the gravel
path a slash of moon all this means
that "liberal humanism is
suburban ideology"
but o my dear since we are mad:
my final word for you is green.

Albumleaves for Madmen: Relics of a Plum-Filled Garden

I

Here most crucially grasps mind wind
rounding to shape this body sun
shading the flesh as it passes
or with snow in its wake razing
no raising putting in relief
white upon white of soul of ice-
like crystals in Zeami's bowl
to some ultimate of flower
—et musicalement se lève—
last night rain on my shingle roof
taught passage from sundown to what
scanning of clouds may be clearing
beyond (most rare preposition)
the marina (Dante's shimmered)
leading to a half-forgotten
image in Mandelstam: basta
theme is plum or by a turning
poplar there's toccata touching
leaf on light on leaf shadows clang
scales of carp in our garden pond
thinking's most twisting inflections
sections of the best of all things
and what is said to gleam at night
this one for instance "Plum Blossoms
by Moonlight" Ma Yüan home coming
from an outing an eternal
competition for the sake of
let us face it poetry stops
dismounts (I postulate a horse)
and retainer in attendance

reflexive ensconces himself
cliffly we imagine winter
at an end black gallows branches
flowers flower spurting from thorns
to view the largest of all whites
to view himself by means of it
to view it viewing him to be
it viewing him miroir profond
miroir and what the hand a stroke
"steadily dragged like a rat's tail"
all this in some formal oval
centuries have burnished its silk.

II

Writing not on in
a surface sense nor
about but inside
other writing ink
knows two at least lives
but more: characters
swell with latent spring
stroke-order of twigs
they speak of themselves
between them spaces
are white are perfume
prismatic castings
while the spray of scroll
the surround is gloss
note exegesis
as if beloved
objects that we touch
by name were merely
aids primers extra-
linear proses
but vernal to verse.

III

I would speak to you (were I not with God: we listen
to the works, the truly posthumous, of Schubert) of
the plum in all the hundred stages of its growing
to this late winter apogee when it and bamboo
and pine are Friends of the Cold Season—as if friends were
of zephyr-climes alone—(but we are mad enough my
dear to know the truth); its jade-bones; how the mountain bends
to man because his passion is the plum; how red plum
(in these doubtful leaping-forward times) and blue-green rock
persist. So I have painted these Three Albumleaves or
Hermits to be linked with you.

Solid real are three notes somebird sings

Solid real are three notes somebird sings
never the same and rocks in water
look maples flatten against wind
salmon leaping up the nightfall
thunder rounds in the valley
river has betrayed its course
read the text of lightning
dead glosses of the moon
nightstare at nothing
glazes the fugue heart
Time Desire
Fog like a tree
rain knouts us
black bridges
mid night-
-alba.

What was it like to have been here?

What was it like to have been here?
  The sun would strike our bodies we
  called it "sun" and we thought us gods
  there were seasons and they changed one
  was spring of dogwood and armies
  of green summer was burning sand
  water was singing you could touch
  fall climbed in light throughout the trees
  winter was snow as white as book.

What was it like to have been?
  Not to know the tenses of
  the verb of verbs "to be" we
  thought had no perfected form
  imperfects in Flaubert or
  Proust we studied talmud-wise
  future was portfolio
  of mutual funds untaxed.

What was it like to have?
  ah but to be possessed,
  to be had! having was
  a simple charm, child's play
  ploy plea having we knew
  ephemeral being
  had Alcibiades.

What was it like to?
  Like to some ghastly
  devotion some ode
  without chorus shot
  through with splendor score
  barless of chaos.

What was it like?
    Con moto like
    Schubert a walk
    down a road night
    falling from trees.

What was it?
    It wasn't
    it merely
    stole being.

What was?
    Sun was.
    Water.

What
Shut
Prime
Rhyme.

Framing is all

Framing is all.
                                        This end-of-day
grey sliced into planks on the porch,
rain bringing to relief design
of pine's arrows suddenly now
sunk back into wood—no—darker
than grey, mauve with aspirations
to black: enough: transcend the porch.
To canal: there's grey for you, sort
of: marred by some tumult of sea-
gulls pursuing what? or merely
arcing to add rotundity
to pure horizontals, nature's
mode of correction (but only
a mode and not binding). Island
beyond, still green but dying, ly-
ing, as though pasted by schoolchild,
on water, green to distract us
from ennui of grey: a live-oak
stunted cover marching away
from Sound wind east to worser fate.
Small white shaft of heron feeding
(imaginary heron there
is no heron: he could be there
but isn't: yet—is it not?—he
strides to preside in his Conclave.)
Above so banal trees masses
cloudgrey worth of course a life of
seeing to seize.
                                        Framing is all.

Twelve Octets

I

. . . More's letters and the end of sun
divisiones aquarum
some merrily (as he would say)
sublimated into very
regnant circularity, some
low-lying seeking eastern shades
God help us the sound is silent
beyond a nothing land is noise.

II

Variations of the waters
let this be study, oblation
words are nearly dead to do it
yet what would you? (painting, cadence
might, dance freed of its body might,
or hacking-off of surplus stone)
only words since words began it
at hand as martyrs to ruin.

III

This gentle other, brother, now
almost in apotheosis
in good faith makes a god of stone
tribal words translating backwards
to Racine, eclogue, or despair.
We shared—friends do this—a silence.
His *"Poésie, si ce mot est*
dicible" taught ethos and terror.

IV

Years now eyes have figured water
to what end but end and its or
other's *(wozu Dichter)* stillness
peals reels gull above the channel
speakless yet scripting to who read:
my arabesques illuminate
no parchment folio nor need
your gloss: sheer moving is design.

V

Rarer since we have blighted it
its red contingent on our whim
soles occidere possunt
poets as the man says venture
verse and its numbers reckon truth
rhyming rhymes something with something
calls this to necessary that
meter measures stanzas to rooms.

VI

Walk blind as if blind through the house
accumulating fable. On
table from beyond a window
light no longer winds walk blindly
for even number fails us numbed
through the house wind will come on us
this mostly night wind from the West
on water over deep water.

VII

Self of sun is birthing to it
(no) sun has no self but wording
(no) were we wordless it is there
only there for words to call it
"hanging around" waiting for words
(no) waiting for only love-like words
like "sun": then see it wag its tail
(no) (yes) or (both of the above).

VIII

That's not the point: the point is why
we care. Black care horsed behind us
Erlkönig cantata world songs
serious music makes us care
for friends parting in Tang mountains
its silence terminal its means
museum fragile. And meaning
nothing and what there is of all.

IX

All merely talk. That doesn't "mean."
And "all"—what is this "all"? Talk blinds.
("Blinds" as the worldly hero blinds
the Cyclops, blinds where birds are shot,
blinds to segment blinds to filter
out the fullest force of setting
eye destruction uttermost glare
of other staring at our pen.)

X

Fog more than it hides unconceals
what's left of day comes burrowing
seeing is close to eye hearing
small hollowed chamber fingers stroke
a bounded self skin's little light
its are the other senses it
will scent me out of raw cover
will lick me clean of dried sun salt.

XI

A ne pas croire and every day
Turner on my right hand rages
on my left Vermeer of deft rest
wind is their only common bond
or eye or spirit or fulcrum
initiating as they say
bipolar intersubjective
nonsoliloquous discoursing.

XII

Writing is righting a riting
no? or phallocentric *vice so-*
litaire? conniving with abyss?
nefas nefandum calling up
some shameful presence? like a "love"
your voice if it fall black returns
impromptu of you beyond waves
o and sun rises with your face. . . .

For Saigyō

michi no be ni	Shade of willow
shimizu nagaruru	flows lucid water
yanagi kana	beside the road:
shibashi tote koso	I stopped (I thought)
tachidomaritsure	only for a while.

Translating seasons
at almost end of winter
oaks stand for willow
but road through woods seduces
stream there is beside
God or whoever else knows
work to be done waits
staff in hand I hesitate
providentially
or by sheerest chance a bench
worm-eaten totters
but holds me I stipulate
for shortest of whiles
knowing the wiles too well of
water full of sun-
light unveils cliffs in the depths
fish like fountain-coins
colors only movement makes
nuances of speed
key-changes where rocks are dam
all this at hill's foot
above snow stained by iron
plant-shoots various
birds wonderfully signing
tracks as who should say
of deer their leaps beyond mind
no: mine sees this bush

as Rilke's hazel *wenn ein*
Glückliches fällt up-
wards some midbranch pinecone shapes
last year's form quartets
catkins saffroned like Buddhist
bonzes in trios
new buds in solid claret
branch I have broken
carry at eye-height stumble
up path look at branch
stumble think how in evening
propped in window frame
it will grace us. As it does.

Sonus

A circle above a line
equipoised in counterpoint
mesh portending merger joint
chaos be it anodyne
some minimal forgetting
lasting Defects of the Sun
modal in distraction stun
the water less abetting
what is now upon us black
or soon to be wind-chanted
threnody: look gulls' wings slack
to shadow pivot slanted
greywards wavewards chaconne: see
gulfing of cacophony.

Three Octaves for Setting

I

River waterclock strikes dark
will fog be bird in day's light?
Lamp falls quiet on paper
cicadas rise to anthem;
Long hours long wakefulness
brief lines in smallest of lives;
Ardent Chapel black on white
second-best or haply first.

II

Green hallows us hollows us
us like the sun at midday;
Wind wrenches river off course
rage uproots oaks of grieving;
Hawks dissolve in gyration
soarings from heartland retrenched;
Rain is Heir Apparent Crown
Prince Emperor of Within.

III

Friend understand my music
here rounded by hills of tombs;
Color passion of our sight
measure frenzy to the touch;
Taste the moon's brutality
smell the smoke of departure;
Insomniac horizon
music understand my friend.

Tenebrae Service

A

Solace river still there *Silberlied*
whose heirs we are he said or should be
drink of it read through it write with it

B

Black beyond, body hill's thighs invite
chest's curve crushes each your every lust
shoulders shine in sun like ruin yours

C

Revel in the color nearly lost
white of birch into grey dissolving
of springsmokeskin sloughed off by waters

D

Mind tells its beads of dread after dread
eye more often stares at single wall
is there heart is there another beat

E

Placing in placing on of whose hands
from without a movement would be boon
would most inwardly the still lake still

F

Said Keats "the feel of not to feel it"
yes but Wordsworth who would ever guess
"all our woes their sad et ceteras"

G

Extract from fearful *Winterreise*
    late in that fateful year some cadence
    Lindenbaum some bird some fountain's fall

H

All was play with him angelic play
    frenzy of sameness madly diverse
    variation raised him next to God

I

Hear the thick the density around
    no sound quickens no ear is tensing
    dark Arcady cities' widowhood.

A *Waka* for a Friend

There will be no end

birthed by letter clock
by Celan at dawn
what poembirds from far
island cloister nave
Komm, schwimmendes Licht
no: but light would save
and by o iris!
so much itself-Thing
like what purple means
as if the last were
it but enough were
Kommst du, schwimmendes
Licht? as though were eye
to stop hand to stop
all just barely here
(note) but if they stopped
by a day in earth
in sun within wind
by lute playing white
"jade engenders smoke"
if music's had there
need no other else
and an iris-poem
and the all of time
look my dear see there
breasting whatever
breakers on lost sand
Kommst du nun, schwimmen-
des Licht? iris sea

Of tears.

Sonus

Let us attend to red while there is time
still time Kirkpatrick memorizing Bach
before he goes blind. Our red too fends off a
black layered thick as though a hand had
flung it there and every year I see it gain
more ground every year red shrinks back
as though black's touch were vile.
And yet like panther-skin this
black how serried of how many
blacks composed how textured. No:
it was of red we spoke: it is window
frame, the window black, white across
silk white across the
top: at the bottom smallest of green.

Poem: For a Gift

. . . this whole corner of the room igniting
as though they had been painted by Van Gogh
the sun's a simple sketch its day's a
minor luster in comparison
to this ice-
melting light but how not weary
no but how translated upwards to the tops
of larches dry all set to burn
to north not west set-over traduced
betrayed transported relics of a saint
or to the new behind the hemlock fence
as yet untreated or to this table where
their dust still lies as though it were
the pigment giving them necessity
a crucialness that things would not
be right not full not totally
done without them more than myths
would do Pactolus Potosí
now are they extinguished
a lesser version/vision from and of
the sound we yearly hear more clearly
the steps we stagger more than stride
Wozu Dichter to teach us how
to count with Helios onetwothree and
does it end here cove inlet anchoring place
not grandiose but grand like late
quartets late sonatas view of Delft
corruptible
yellow
incorruptible.

Prelude, Variations, and Finale on "The Sufferings of Light"

I. Prelude

Fear only slightly words
with light or just in time
will come come like colors

II. Variations

i

High T'ang moth on my hand
grey silks carefully flung
over a Gaudí screen
live amber through shining
sail triangular striped
veined crisscrossed slated tiled
mosaic beyond sight
but quaking but breathing
probing the flesh of palm
as if it were as if

ii

Erlösung high in trees
resolution before
fall look westwards chorale
homelike virtues bourgeois
accountability
gold at the bottom line
(no: top) cedar waxwings
slashing ochre through dark
punning light on cedars
branch calls bird calls branch calls

iii

Monstrous crime in the hills
river of dried blood stems
from it serpentwise or
now a sun reviving
sheeningly Potosí
or—this is endless—or
load of likenesses mined
last sole vast master vein
by which we are led goaled
by which we are galled gulled

iv

Sun "comes up" belying
fact "sunrise" apes Versailles
"sunlight" redundancy
sun's money-grasping fist
then be it French prelude's
notes inégales flakes
filter down from cosmic
Carrara temple beam
millions for sunflowers
Heidegger's peasant shoes

v

Will words from well well up
despite narcissus face
look meaning I mean look
this is pond this maple
this bridge this source of light
these are most common fish
signifying but fish
if this to madness led
instead of bleak ennui
black ennui *noir en nuit*

vi

Blessing muses *Segen*
Sinnt from unremembrance
Lethe springs such clearing
we behind tapestry
are its threads warp and woof
sun beyond our textile
leads through it to water
to what we do should might know
take comfort in your cave
moss lures from stone to stone

vii

Day congealing to stone
to stones in legion here
nothing there is not they
our rage for excess for
sheer inutility
for superfluity
aesthetic ascetic
drives us to honing them
hewing them to folly
of bevel and polish

viii

Love it is love of them
goads us to terraces
aqueducts labyrinths
ladders to holy heights
sculpted trails to other
willfully unfinished
(because redundancy
is godhead) sites for Sun
is incarnate in rock
in hardly abiding

ix

Yet noonpoint reasoned light
Descartes' high mirador
midi justesse justice
blocks words we would align
reducing luxury
softening rectangles
to curves serving purpose
none to maternal line
to sinuosity
massively outrageous

x

Volcanoes march to south
beside our road to poor
rich authenticity
new-plastered swept to bone
to honor morning smoke
prismatic of all greys
gold torn off by Conquest
walls sliced of their silver
rock residue remains
setting for mountains' ash

xi

Fortress sacred virgins
last frenzied encampment
meditation aerie
concubinage royal
weather-station Greenwich
lengthening sun shadows
crops and when to plant them
no all no: here sheer Work
erects itself around
unworked and supple stone

xii

Cusp cup cupola this
and fog layering it
beggaring belief site
wintering all summer
ultimate rose final
canticle Andes-wrapped
crater (or who should say):
or: ground flashes fires
concavity of smoke
circles upwards to snow

xiii

Let us manfully face
aporia impasse
old "ambiguity"
margins tenuousness
creeping diffusiveness
to wit (wit has limits):
what other would you have?
color eschews meaning
poems quake out of meaning
even so trace of stones

xiv

Late August rain forebodes
and is foreboding light's
demise to every heath
its Lear hear by lightning
read the text of colors
grey to black chromatics
smell how darkness thickens
taste its familiar, fog,
touch with whatever hands
its so forgotten face.

III. Finale

Conjecture gave it birth;
words have their play, their give;
vowels, shiftings; icons live
capriciously, their worth

is all in spawn, in spread;
presence, insistence flee.
Stones at least persist: see
sun bleeds in them who bled.

Yet ours is work of black-
ness: how to mist turn sound?
(temple rises from ground
while city doubles back):

Dearth, opulent of sense,
muse on this innocence.

William H. Matheson became professor and visiting chair of comparative literature at Washington University in St. Louis in 1970 and continued to teach in that program until his retirement in 1996. He has also taught at Yale, Tufts, and Brandeis, as well as at the University of Michigan, where he earned his Ph.D. in French. He is the author of *Claudel and Aeschylus: A Study of Claudel's Translation of the "Oresteia"* and the coauthor of *Pindar: Selected Odes* and of *Toward a Modern Japanese Poetry.* He has also published a number of scholarly monographs and articles.

Matheson's poetry and translations have appeared in *River Styx*, *Webster Review*, *The Avant-Garde Today*, and *One Hundred Frogs.* He has been a frequent contributor to *Anthology,* a series of poetry collections published by Ikuta Press in Kobe, Japan. A limited edition of *Tung Ch'i-Ch'ang's Album*—a poem in eight sections, inspired by an album of eight paintings by an artist of the Ming period—was published in 1995.

J. Thomas Rimer, professor and chair of the Department of East Asian Languages and Literatures at the University of Pittsburgh, has written widely on various aspects of Japanese literature, art, and culture.

My thanks to Gordon and Elizabeth Orear, J. Thomas Rimer, Linda Peavy and Ursula Smith, Robert Hegel, Emma Kafalenos, Marvin Marcus, and my colleagues at Washington University.

W.H.M.